To Start Believing...the panic attacks - beginning and end

Mariyana Doykova

Published by Mariyana Doykova, 2020.

Table of Contents

Mariyana Doykova

TO START BELIEVING...
The Panic Attacks – Beginning and End

Panic – the End of Everything and the Beginning of Something New

VEGETATIVE CRISIS. Have you heard about something like that? And have you experienced such a feeling? I suppose you have. If you have decided to open the present modest literary work, it means you have experienced crisis or you are still experiencing it. Vegetative crisis. This is the other name for the term **PANIC ATTACK.**

Perhaps you have already made all possible tests and you have found you are clinically healthy. It is the first and the most common reaction, when panic befalls a normal person. He scampers to the medics to find explanation for the fear of the loss of control over his body that has suddenly oppressed him and the strange accompanying symptoms. Rejecting number of other illnesses, you have gotten to the conclusion you suffer from panic attacks. I deliberately use the word „suffering", because you are not ill but suffer from **emotional discomfort** that you purposefully experience.

The vegetative crisis and its symptoms appear unexpectedly for the person. The peak of the panic attack comes in 10 minutes. After the attack's end you feel general weakness, drowsiness, after which all returns to the normal daily round without any consequences.

Vegetative crisis – a form of vegetative-vascular dystonia that manifests in the form of groundless anxiety and fear.

The word „crisis" indicates the body hasn't adequately reacted to a situation, which is critical, stressing for it. It is not obligatory an outside factor – sometimes the vegetative crisis appears out of nowhere. In any case, this is body's vegetative functions fault with the participation of the cardiovascular system.

You have experienced a traumatic event that hasn't found its answer and solution. You haven't had strategy for coping with this emotion, you haven't found a way out and support. The body has retained this emotion and the dark thoughts and feelings have turned into reaction that has created a negative conviction and has sunk in the unconsciousness. The brain hasn't coped with the situation and has blocked at that very moment, that's why the event continues to happen again and again. The thoughts are entirely directed towards how you would eventually cope if the crisis comes over again. Or, more precisely, how you wouldn't cope because one feels powerless in such a situation. You take into your head that if you haven't managed once, the event would happen similarly the next time. You appear into impasse and you don't look for solution in your mind but fight against yourself only. The fight is for avoiding the panic attack in order not to be made to appear in the trap of fear for another time. The more you think on how not to let the attack happen again, the more you are attracted by it.

The vegetative crisis is an extreme form of ***vegetative-vascular dystonia,*** more popular as ***panic attack*** or ***panic crisis,*** as far as it is mainly caused by panic disorders, neuroses. Groundless fear and anxiety are their major symptoms.

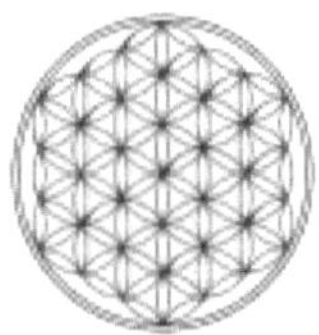

Stress and Fear

One suffers a very severe stress, when the panic attack happens. He fears the repetition of the condition he provokes himself, on the background of the least unfavourable factors. A new panic attack might start as a result of the fact the person is in an unknown environment, while being in closed space, when threatened by an assault or another type of punishment. All this is solely caused by the fear, by the stress you've been subject to. When you are in a hostile atmosphere and under stress, you start thinking only about that. The heart starts beating at high speed and you start worrying about the next thing that is going to happen. Your body switches to a programme of surviving, fighting against the imaginary enemy. You are expecting the worst. Your thoughts are directed solely to the past episodes of this attack, and your unconsciousness has retained the feeling of fear. Each time you think about that trauma, you produce the same emotions in the body as if you are experiencing it again.

_______________To start believing...

You literally live in the past and fear it not to repeat in the future. You ramble between past and future and the key to solving the problem is to focus on the present. ***The fear does not originate from the present moment.*** It originates from your past contact with it. You constantly think about the emotion as far as it was far strong. Is it possible to stop thinking about the fear and to just accept that it has happened? ***Awareness, acceptance and will for change*** are the few steps towards freedom. Are you afraid of that moment? While you are reading the present work? If you are concentrated on the process you are accomplishing at the moment – then there is nothing to be afraid of. But, if you otherwise feel fear – it means your thoughts are somewhere else and you don't realize that there is no actual threat existing at every moment. The threat might have passed or you might expect it coming in some time. But not at the present moment.

People stop paying attention to the nice things that have happened to them, but focus on that very thing that causes them suffering. And this is how their whole life passes – in expectation of „the bad" thing to repeat again and again. As far as you constantly expect that thing, you unconsciously look for that memory, that familiar thing, which has preserved as a picture in your unconscious. And when you find it – BOOM! The fear, the stress, the emotion pounce on you again.

That's why passing by somewhere you have gotten a panic attack or meeting a person – the retained emotion emerges in your mind right away. This would continue until you decide to put it to an end and to change the established habits in your unconscious.

Your state of mind should change in order to change the circumstances. Suffering comes, when you think you are dependent on external circumstances. You are not! You are dependent on your own thoughts. ***Change your thinking in order to change your life.*** We don't attract what we want but what we are. If your entire consciousness is seized by fear and you long for something nice at the same moment – this cannot come true. You would attract only fearful situations because this is what you are unconsciously looking for. We are constantly resisting the fear consequence, while deeply keeping the reason for it into ourselves. ***Fear disappears, when we accept it and exchange it for another feeling.*** When we redirect our thoughts. This process takes time and needs faith. Thoughts turn into habits and the habits build your circumstantial environment, your real world.

Only pure consciousness can influence reality. Reality is the sort we create. ***Consciousness clears, when you accept your past, do not think about the future and focus on the present moment.***

Forget about the other people, about the circumstances, problems, time and everything. Accept the things that happened in your past and learn how to be grateful for everything. When you start feeling gratitude, love, appreciation and care, then your heart would normalize its rhythm. Take a break. From everything and everybody. *Take some time for yourself, for overcoming the trauma.* What happened years ago, doesn't matter. Yesterday is also past, together with the emotions that have been experienced. Don't misuse these past emotions by prancing them repeatedly in your mind. They are past. Everything that has happened, has been in favour of you. Even „the bad" things, because consequently it turns out they have helped you reaching new information, to undertake new actions, to change yourself and all that with one and only purpose – your better existence on Earth.

When you are disappointed, under pressure or live with disturbing emotions, you start analyzing yourself. The heartbeat gets out of its usual rhythm, the brain is confused and the situation might only get worse. When the heart does not beat within the rhythm, the brain switches off. And when the heart calms down, the vibrations the whole body starts producing, form a magnetic field. This magnetic field is energy, and energy is frequency that transmits information. The same energy transmits thought, too.

This is the reason for what we think to turn into our reality. The sense of guilt, fear and the energy of suffering cannot be transmitted by thoughts of health and happiness. These are different energies. All of you have experienced feeling negative energy from a person or when a particular space is filled with it. If your heart is sinking, if you experience anxiety and fear, then the next doze of the same is coming for you. You radiate what you feel and respectively you attract more of it.

The panic attack itself is not dangerous for your health, but is frequent manifestation leads to serious complications. People start developing many and various **phobias**: some are afraid of death, other – of closed space, etc. Often, the springing up autonomous crises might provoke cardiac dysfunctions leading to blood pressure sharp fluctuations. Also, digestive and nervous systems problems might develop on their grounds. If the digestive system stops functioning normally, it influences the brain activity.

The fear of next crisis might affect person's social skills. Many people try to limit their living space, to more rarely appear in public, and as a result, communicativeness fades, consciousness blurs and inappropriate behaviour might unfold.

Each vegetative crisis occurs because of the fact that great quantity of norepinephrine, adrenaline, steroid hormones, acetylcholine and other substances accumulate in the organism. One should be aware the crisis manifests different way with each person as far as each organism is different. Despite that, modern medicine classifies „the attack" in several types.

Mainly stress and psychological anomalies are the major reason for the development of vegetative-vascular dystonia. ***Each vegetative crisis*** occurs unexpectedly and sharply but ***does not appear to be a threat for human life***. And this is the first thing one should learn. Beside the entire clinical picture and no matter how awful it could be, you just remember one rule – ***nobody dies of panic attack***.

The accumulation of various types of stress and the suppression of emotions are the psychological cause for an attack. When a person does not let the emotions get out and keeps everything inside him, it threats to cause crisis. It doesn't matter what type of emotions you maintain – positive or negative. The important is to live them through, not to reject them but to take them out. ***If you keep this status inside yourself for a long time, you risk to get a panic attack.***

I used to do just the same, too. I didn't express emotions, gulped a lot of things and got angry inside myself. All I had to speak out and express against somebody else I directed inside towards myself. I reiterated past moments, insults and anger. I punished myself for someone else's words and actions and accepted all the negative energy in my soul, which piled up with passing the truths over in silence.

I recently thought over the thousands of things that happen to us and got to the conclusion that *fear is stronger than any other emotion. Than love, for example.* Namely love should prevail and lead us along the unknown roads. We build as personalities and become better people through its power. Each person looks for and needs love, even those, who claim they can live without it. The lack of love or its manifestations makes us pent up, uncertain, insecure and bitter. Then fear creeps in silently in our soul, captures it gradually and the moment it takes possession of us comes. There is a trick, of course. This notorious love everybody looks for somewhere and from somebody is actually inside each person. If you don't find love in yourself, there is no way someone to hand it to you on a platter. Since you don't radiate love, there is no way to attract it. *You should first love yourself with all your shortcomings you are aware of.* You are able to change what you don't like. Human is a unique creation.

I can't stop admire the way the body is organized and how all things in it interact perfectly.

Living in fear is difficult. To live *in fear from the fear itself* is even more difficult. We start trying to control people, situations. This is impossible. The only thing we can control is our mind. The faster you start changing your habits, the faster you'll start living in happiness. ***Panic attacks frequency is due to our fear for them not to repeat again***. It accumulates inside us periodically and reaches its peak at a certain moment. ***Each person, even the one with the most unstable psyche, could cope with the stressful states.*** Desire, awareness, support and change of lifestyle are necessary. The road is hard but we'll walk it by small steps. Since I made it, you can do it, too. Only wish for it! Now it is our time to live, to enjoy and to share love! ***There is no before, there is no after. All is now.*** Start focusing on present the sooner possible, because there is no future without present. What you do at the moment, what you think about at the moment, the choice you constantly make, defines your future. Did you realize already that everything happens now, at this very moment? After that, this very moment is past and you outline your future with your next act in the present.

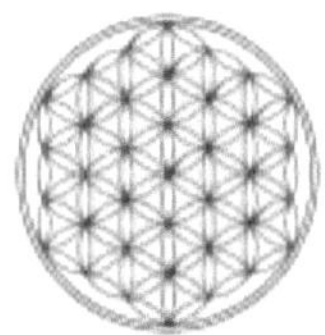

After the Attacks

Forget your previous life before the panic attacks. Forget your previous consciousness, your previous impulses and way of life. After you've lived the attacks through, get aware that the time for something new has come. This new thing is You. They have happened to you because your body screams for change. Listen to it and understand it. Be merciful and self-indulgent to yourself. It's time for you to build yourself, to analyze, to get deep and to find your forgotten Self. It's time to start living. You won't cope with their manifestations until you don't find the will to rethink your actions. All depends on you and your desire for change. There is nobody else to help, if you don't do it for yourself. Someone might support you, direct you, but *the change swarms from your consciousness only*. This could happen through faith. *Faith is clear defining of the goal.* The goal is to define what you want and what way you'd like to realize it. Take a look back to your past, see what used to hurt you,

what suppressed your emotions, how many insults you gulped, how many times you kept silent while you had to speak out. How many times you felt unnecessary, insufficient, uneducated and wicked? What secretly used to hurt you and accumulated negative impulses in your mind is already escalating. It emerged on the surface. It comes up across your body in the form of adrenaline and puts you on your knees in front of your own impotence. So, the moment to get to know yourself and to start new life has come. Welcome!

Take a deep breath, look around – life is going on. Flowers smell sweet, trees come into leaf, birds sing. Do you hear them? You don't, do you? You only hear the frequented beats of your heart. And you are right. You hear them because you are alive! You won't die, at least not now. ***You are not ill, you are not insane, you are not alone!*** The people, who have experienced the same as us around the world, are a lot. And none of them has died during a panic attack. Reject fear, inconvenience, reduce anxiety, master your consciousness and concentrate.

It is fair to specify that I haven't got a doctor's degree, I am not a trained psychologist and I do not pretend for scientific knowledge. All written in the present book is based on my personal experience, meetings with people and a lot of read articles on psychic disorders topic. I decided to write down what I learned and experienced in order to charge you with hope and peace that there is way out. Give yourself time and use your will in order to start believing in success.

Even a lot of negative has happened to you up to now, turn of circumstances exists. You would need ***faith, tenacity and desire***.

I just recently graduated Law and I am already jurist according to the documents. This was another dream of mine that came true. Time will tell whether I'd use the education for professional development or will turn to another field.

Psychology is far more interesting to me but as of now I have no possibility of starting training in another field. I am 37 years old, I have gone through many adversities, I got to know myself and continue doing it. I changed some things in my daily life, I got aware of some others from my past and I go on dreaming. I have ideas, goals, confidence and gratitude. Gratitude for everything that has happened to me and continues happening. I look only ahead, not back. I learned to see the signs, to be patient and not to get angry about the things that do not happen the way I figured them. It is always for our good when something is taken from us or another thing is impossible to come true. Always. In any case. Even if you are very angry with something at the moment, we realize after that that it had to happen just this way. And if you are observant well enough, you'd see also the reason for a particular event /desire, dream, longing/ not to come true the way you had expected. Everything has its explanation but sometimes we get it in a while.

I am sure everybody that has opened the present book, has experienced our common problem – the panic attack. Otherwise it's useless to read because you wouldn't understand anything. Although there could be bored masochists, who'd be eager to read about that extreme feeling of fear.

And mentioning the word fear... this is emotional condition, expressionless feeling, which paralyzes us and makes our mind draw creepy scenarios and death statuses. This is the base of each panic attack. The star number in the performance! To root our body by illusory fear and to ruin our life. Nasty, isn't it? Unfortunately, it is just this way. If you don't get yourself together and don't calm your mind, you'd surely be under the influence of these attacks for a long time and this would seize your life rhythm in any aspect.

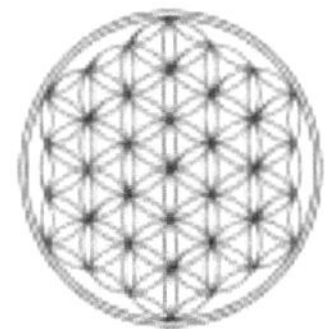

To Cope with Discomfort

I suggest us to get to work and overcome ourselves in order to try ad cope with discomfort the attacks cause. You know very well they come suddenly. They do not ask, do not wait, do not consider. They hit instantly and stiffen us. Each one of us remembers pretty well the first time it happened to him. This is where the problem is, that you remember pretty well where the panic attack has happened. You don't stop thinking about that and experience the stress repeatedly. What a wonderful, unforgettable experience! Not only once, of course, but every time you get into the known situation. It never happens only once, then they start repeating, sometimes even too often. You shouldn't allow them becoming part of your daily life and shouldn't allow everything to be centered around the fear of a panic attack. ***Fear provokes fear.*** You have to find a way to control yourself in order to reduce their intensity in the course of time, until they start fading away for long period of time. There is no place for deceiving ourselves – they do not

disappear at once, but it's far easier to cope with it, when you know what you face. Some people become dependant on that feeling and even if it is negative, it acts on them as a drug. They determine themselves through it and it is very difficult to detach from the fear. The pills, the so called anti-depressants, do not cure this condition. They only mask the symptoms and make your body become addicted to them. The miracle does not happen by trials to treat the symptoms but after finding the cause and start working on its removal. The feeling something helps, makes us constantly reach for it. You should find exactly "such thing" and use it in case you start feeling a coming panic attack. Many people may disprove me for the medicines' effect. I won't argue with them, who needs, has to take them but I firmly rejected doing it because I didn't want to become dependent and to master my psychic condition with pill the whole my life. I am far young, far strong and I don't want to depend on anybody or anything, I know I can count on myself. You can't wait someone or something to cure you. You can't wait and stay impassive. *Life is in your hands.* The point you have taken a pill is not accepted as effort for change. This is rather suppression of the state and its time postponing. This is time you waste in hopes instead of using it to act. *Passive waiting for the result is not solution of the problem.* Since you don't actively participate in the fight,

it is doomed to failure. And neither luck, nor hope would complete your task. You would be happy to get recovery but meanwhile you wait. And what are your vibes, mien, expression? As of an ill wretch? And why do you do it? Because the others do it? Or because you've heard this is the way you have to react? Thus you get into a vicious circle and when the state turns being chronic, the mission to get out of it seems lost.

You act completely normally from common sense's point of view. But common sense just keeps what is already created. It is associated with logic and the latter – with the facts. In this case, have we factually recovered? Do we feel as recovered or as ill? Beside we feel as ill, we don't see a way out. So, how a doctor to help you as far as you are in a union with the illness? There is no place for doubt and hope, because months and years will pass with them and the chance for curing would reduce as far as the illness would penetrate more and more in the consciousness and into each cell of the body. Grab the faith by the throat and squeeze tightly until you feel it in your veins. Faith and confidence will change you.

Let us make difference between anxiety attack and panic attack.

Panic attacks come suddenly and include intensive and often creepy fear. They are accompanied by startling physical symptoms, such as frequented cardiac rhythm,

asthma or nausea. They happen without obvious cause and appear suddenly.

Anxiety attacks include anxiety, stress and fear. Anxiety is usually connected with anticipation of a stressful situation, experience or event. It could occur gradually.

Anxiety is also connected with something, perceived as stressful or threatening. Panic attacks aren't always caused by stressors and most often occur as if out of nothing.

Panic attacks usually cause embarrassments and fears connected with anticipation of new attacks. This leads to avoiding places or situations, where you consider you could be exposed to risk of attack.

I will tell you about my handbook, will also describe for you few suggestions you should obligatory try with yourself. There should be something to make ***your brain get over the illusory threat***. The fear you experience is ungrounded and you are not exposed to any risk, except the one of spoiling your life. I succeeded to cope with and overcome the fear solely by change of thoughts and I am sure this is great decision that would exercise beneficial influence on you, your close ones and the surrounding environment. Becoming aware of what happens, you have to make decision for change, to thank for this miraculous gift that had

been given, in order to look into your soul and to understand you don't go in the right direction. All bad things happening to us are not AGAINST us but FOR us.

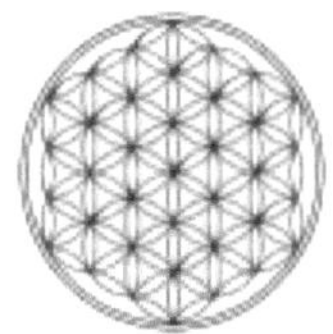

Few Words about Me

It is time to tell you about my beginning, straight about the new stage in my life and how I sharply jumped into it.

I want to specify in the beginning that I was quite fearless person, even carelessly reckless. I loved risk and the feeling of adrenaline rising in my body. High speed, bungee jumps, extreme merry-go-rounds, parachute jumping... all these pleasures purposefully looked for by me. I remember once going to Sofia by bus in order to go and jump from the highest bridge they allowed bungee jumps from. The other places looked to me amateur's. Anyway, my point is that the feeling of fear was completely unknown to me.

I have always considered myself also a person, who controls himself as well as the situations. The lack of control used to drive me crazy. Everything had to be preliminary measured, outlined and I to have few B-plans if something was to go wrong. That used to bring kind of calmness in my stirred soul. My zodiac sign is Scorpio.

I am not quite an astrological fanatic, but out of my social meetings I got the conclusion there are similar characteristics within the representatives of zodiac signs. Composure is one of my inborn features.

I participated in a car crash in my younger years, where I was physically unhurt but it left a lasting mark in my mind. I felt fear for the first time and realized I am not immortal, and that misfortune might overtake at any moment. I quickly shook the negative feeling off and my life went on the usual way.

Few years after the car accident, I was with a big company in the mountains and one day it happened so that I went skiing on my own. Generally I like being on my own and very often I even strive for it. The surrounding people burden me many times, may be because they don't understand me or I don't give them a chance to do it. Everything during that day went great (according to the plan, as it is said), until, at one beautiful moment, flying over the skiing track, I came onto a stone that turned me over and I hurt my leg badly. I still keep a memory in the shape of a scar.

Later the same day, before going to dinner, I started sweating and becoming dizzy. I thought I have raised temperature and I was getting ill. Actually, I didn't have temperature but I went to bed for a rest. In an hour I felt better and

went down for dinner with the others.

About a year passed from this event and I had already forgotten it. I had an appointment with my gynecologist as far as I had great desire to get pregnant, but things didn't happen at once the way I supposed. I have always had the attitude that when I decide to have children, it would happen right away. Alas, several months passed but the good news for pregnancy didn't come around. That's why I started visiting the gynecologist often, making any kinds of examinations and continuing anticipating the happy event. Failures in this field are quite stressful for a woman, may be leading to kind of depression. Every month I was expecting with thrill the positive result and when it didn't come, I broke down but hope didn't leave me.

As far as I had some time till the meeting with the gynecologist, I made my way shopping some items for home. I loved driving, feeling conveniently and comfortably in my car. I remember I had stopped at traffic lights I used to pass by number of times a day. While waiting for the green light, I suddenly felt unwell, I started gasping for breath, I just couldn't take breath. I opened the car window for air to get in and some persistent thoughts rushed into my head... how I am going to faint any moment, I started feeling dizzy and was not able to see anything in front of me. The thought something bad would happen any moment, started alarming me even more. The whole that emotion evolved very quickly, it straightly burst in

my mind, while not more than 20-30 seconds had passed. The green light came and I continued on my way barely. Starting from the traffic lights, I somewhat calmed down as far as I was not in a trap anymore

– this is how I felt in the middle of the small crossroad. I reached the store and got off for shopping. Suddenly, my legs softened, I again started feeling the constriction and lost balance for a moment. I leaned on the shopping cart and went numb. I couldn't move, I was not aware what was happening and what to do. I felt squirmed from the surrounding ones. My vision blurred, I had rapid heartbeat, burden in my chest and constriction. I was afraid I was dying and didn't know what to do. I was terribly afraid. I stood for some time leaned on to the cart and after this burst of emotions somewhat faded, I nerved myself and left. I went directly to the gynecologist's. There I felt in secure place. I knew somebody competent would help me if I faint or lose consciousness. This thought calmed me down. I told the doctor about the incident. He decided my blood pressure dropped, made me lie for a while and brought some Ayran /yogurt-based beverage/ for me. In some 30 minutes I felt better and went home. The worry I am ill of something wasn't leaving me. I didn't have another explanation about what happened with me. I thought constantly over and the emotion overtook again in the evening. Constriction, trembling, panic, palpitation. I couldn't get from the couch up. I told my partner something bad was happening with me and we have to go to the hospital. No! We had to call for ambulance, I didn't have time to get to the hospital... something bad would happen to me any moment! He said there is nothing wrong with me, that I am conceited and that we'd call ambulance if I faint. I was just like paralyzed. I hardly collected myself to go to the bed and lied down. I tried to sleep but it was impossible. I would die any moment! I was terribly afraid. I was trembling, I was already feeling real heaviness in the chest and didn't dare to move from the fright. I don't remember exactly how I spent that night, but I was in good shape in the morning and started to my GP's. I told her I have difficulties with breathing, heaviness in the chest, perhaps a cardiac problem and I need examinations because, for God's sake!, I didn't have much time left. I felt as if on the verge of death, or rather that annoying woman is stalking for me at any corner. I had fallen into the ferocious trap of the illusion that I would collapse at any moment and this wretched life would come to its end.

At the doctor's, they measured my blood pressure, they examined my breathing and heart. They didn't find anything except increased heart rate. I persisted for more detailed examinations because there had to be health cause for all that (at least this is what I considered in the beginning). The fact I didn't know what caused my state, turned me right away in the swirl of panic. I got referral for neurologist at my insistence. I started right away because

I felt awfully terrible and wanted the reason for my death suffering to be found as soon as possible. I was walking, alone, I was unable to drive a car. Everything was happening before my eyes as if at slow-motion. People, streets, vehicles... I was seeing blurred, my heart was beating madly and I could hardly take breath. It seemed to me I would collapse on the ground any moment. I reached the doctor's, entered, and directly described the symptoms in order not to waste time. They scanned my head, assured me there was nothing worrying and saw me off. Shock! That lack of diagnosis didn't bring me any relief. I got back to my GP, who is also an acquaintance of mine as far as we are neighbours by residence. I showed her the test and insisted for additional ones as far as I was sure there was a problem with me and we needed to define it. Each minute was precious for me because... people... I was dying from inside and was expecting the worst to happen with my beautiful existence any moment. The doctor obviously understood what was happening, she didn't tell me anything but prescribed medicines I had to take according to a scheme. She mentioned something about the nerves, I think, but at the moment of affect I hardly remembered anything. I grabbed the prescription and decided to get home first, to lie down for a while and to try to calm down. It was perhaps time to decide which clothes to prepare for my own funeral, if I had the time for that, of course.

I sat on the couch and the fear had escalated to the utmost. The fact they didn't find any illness worried me even more as far as I didn't have prescribed treatment. This is one of the paradoxes with these states, I jokingly look at today. You know you are pretty right but you continue looking for proof you are ill at the same time. You obviously do not want to be healthy. Instead of calming down, the person continues looking for the suffering. Most probably, because he had decided this way would feel he has taken the control. Control he had lost with the occurrence of the panic attacks.

I took out the medicines prescription to take a look at it and check them on internet what they are prescribed for. I read they were antidepressants. I popped on opinions about the benefits and the disadvantages of them and I was firm I wouldn't buy them. But while reading opinions on the medicines, I found an article that described my symptoms. At once my heart calmed down. I was already aware about the cause for the indisposition happening with me. I had had panic attacks. The next few days I read everything I found on that topic. I understood they were not deadly even though I didn't believe it. I felt better but I still entered the bathroom with the mobile nearby in order to be able to call somebody in case something happened to me. Anyway, I was not facing heart attack, stroke and I didn't suffer cancer disease, at least not detected one.

What I Learnt from What I Read Then

The panic attack is an extreme manifestation of **vegetative-vascular dystonia** (VVD), characterized by nervous system impairing. According to the International Classification of Diseases (ICD), this disease is given code F 41.0 – **panic disorder** or, said in other words, **episodic paroxysmal anxiety**.

The interesting thing is that psychotherapists have established general characteristics of the personality, most pliant to such unpleasant manifestations. Most often these are women (very seldom men), whose personality characterizes by the following features:

artistry;

instability of thinking;

tendency to dramatize situations; constant anticipation of unpleasant moments, fear; inadequate reaction to critics;

constant desire for body improvement.

Apparently such people can get a sudden panic attack, accompanied by the feeling of anxiety and feeling of fear. Alongside, the somatic symptoms are best expressed.

I had almost all of the listed symptoms of panic attack. Perhaps I like the maximum, sadistic loading of the mind. Rapid heartbeat, constriction, dizziness and blurred vision were the most frequent and most sharply expressed. Let us look to these symptoms as sign by our body. Our **heart** starts beating madly because it's time to hear it and start listening to it. Time to calm down, to slow down and to turn to our inner anxiety, to cure ourselves.

To accept **constriction** as something that chokes us and we need to free ourselves from in order to start breathing normally. I associate **dizziness** with the loss of control. We can't control everything around us even if we try to. It is good to concentrate on only one thing and to work on it. Not to distract ourselves too much.

Blurred vision is sign we need to focus. We have stopped seeing the things clearly and refract them through unreal prism. Our vision is blurred, we don't see well, we have lost our direction.

Panic disorder is repeating episodes of intensive irrational fear, panic or anxiety, having the following symptoms:

> Anxiety about something, most often undefined.

> A feeling that something bad would happen.

> Desire for escape.

> Feeling you are losing control, getting crazy, you are losing your mind.

> Feeling you are dying and you are receiving a heart attack.

> Feeling for unreality, known as de-realization and de-personalization.

> Changes in the heartbeat or the pulse – rapid heartbeat, palpitations.

> Changes in breathing – lack of air, constriction, rapid breathing, hyper ventilation.

> Chest pain, discomfort, feeling of breast heaviness (fear of having heart attack).

> Dizziness, feeling of fainting (because of low blood pressure).

> Nausea/stomach problems.

> Formicating/fever/perspiration.

> Weakness in the legs.

› Warm waves.

› Permanent dizziness, staggering, difficulty/inability to walk straight or without support.

___________________To start believing...

At the simultaneous occurrence of three or more of the listed symptoms, we can speak about **panic attack** with great probability. The multiple repetition of panic attacks leads to „chronicity" of the state and is defined as **panic disorder.**

Panic disorder's etiology and ontological nature is not understood to this day.

Panic attacks are organism's attempt to relief from the accumulated over excessive anxiety and signal from the soul for non-symbolic change in our life.

Generalized anxiety lies in the base of panic attacks. And what is anxiety caused by? Irritating factors in our life that are often present there for years. Irritating factors should be looked for in the immediate life environment – marriage or partner, family, work, place of living, social environment, lifestyle... as well as combination of all these.

I searched for my "irritating factor" long time but still, I couldn't define it unconditionally. According to me, the suppressed emotions yet from my childhood lie in the base of my panic attacks. The low self-esteem and the feeling you are constantly intruding yourself on people build protective wall you put your emotions behind. All unsaid things accumulate into you and the moment when this held back negative energy is to break out of the body comes.

I don't suffer lack of confidence at the moment because I perfectly know what I am and what I am capable of. But I suffered low self-esteem since very young age. Have you thought whether it has been the same with you?

Is this behaviour familiar to you?

› You often excuse or say: „I don't want to disturb you", „I don't want to bother you...", „Why to engage you with me...", „Not to burden you with my problems..."

› You difficultly accept favours and gestures from people but you do a lot of these for others.

› If somebody does something for you, you hurry to return the favour.

› You give your turn or the time for yourself because you feel others have more significant problems and more urgent needs.

› When you are with more people you often keep silent, you don't take the floor except if they ask you something.

The feeling that we intrude, we disturb the surroundings, the need to excuse ourselves and the inability to accept gestures are just symptoms of low self-esteem. They look like kindness, good behaviour but this is mask that holds us captives of our old behavioral models. And it is these models that make us feel insignificant, unimportant and not deserving anything. Actually, do you know the word „persona" we use for „personality " (the image with which we present ourselves before the world) comes from Latin and means „mask". Personality is the way surroundings perceive you but it is not the real inner Self of an individual.

It is important to understand you should not put the others' needs before yours own, always to speak out what troubles you, to share your feelings with the close ones, to express opinion and not to suppress, when you feel insulted or hurt. We'll discuss later these needs, too, in order you to understand how important it is your Self to be above pretentions and prejudices. When we speak out everything at the very moment, we close the door to thinking over it thousands of times and to ask ourselves: „What would happen, if..." We leave it in the past and do not go back to that emotion.

A lot of changes happen in one's soul every day, but his way of expressing remains often the same. His ability to clarify himself is lost. The feelings, thoughts and perceptions that are left unspoken or veiled, pile up inside the personality and might lead to psychological collapse. Learn to express yourself correctly.

After finding the cause for my anxiety and that I am not seriously ill, I calmed down to a certain extent. My panic attacks didn't stop but reduced. I started reading a lot on the topic in Bulgarian as well as in English. I wanted to help myself on my own. First, in order not to become dependent on medicines, and second, because I didn't know a close person, who has gotten over that hardship, and I didn't want to receive advices from doctors, who have only studied the state but haven't experienced it. I highly respect their labour but I was looking for another kind of help.

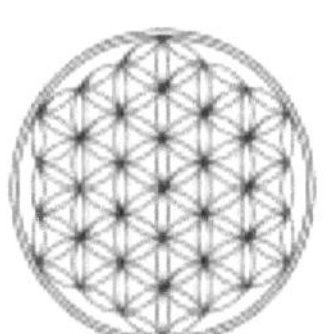

Breathing

I learned that **breathing** is very important part at the occurrence of panic. When we recognize the attack's start, we can prevent it by correct breathing for the panic not to rush in our mind. Those words that each of you has perhaps heard: „calm down, breathe", they are not just words. ***Breathing is at the base of our stable and calm condition***, we only need to learn how to master it. I intend to dash into the depths of meditation for a long time, but I always postpone, because I have decided to go to Bali, India or Tibet. I'd like to obtain knowledge and skills directly from the source.

The understanding of breathing mechanism at panic attack is of key significance for its stopping. Breathing realizes by a muscle placed in the lower part of the chest, the so called diaphragm. It goes down to the abdominal cavity at breathing in, pushing the abdominal organs downwards and inflating the abdomen. The diaphragm contracts and increases the chest volume, creating conditions for air to suck in the lungs. Exhalation is passive process and does not require efforts.

There diaphragm recovers its domed shape and the air is pushed out of the lungs.

Little children and adults in the state of dreaming, breathe according to this mechanism. It supplies great quantities of oxygen without organism's efforts.

The occurrence of anxiety and fear strains the abdominal muscles automatically. This totally excludes the possibility for diaphragm breathing at panic attack. At danger, the organism tightens the abdomen in order to keep the important internal organs secure. The goal is the living creature to save itself and to run away within few seconds to minutes, and during that time it might not breathe effectively. Ineffective breathing in turn, leads to dizziness, constriction, vertigo, darkening before eyes. You know well all these symptoms and have experienced them. These accompany each classic panic attack.

_______________Chest breathing leads to escalation of anxiety and turning on the rest emergency lights in the mind. Fear has already arisen, having strong tangible physical expression – breathing. The mind looks for objective reason for it. A panic attack determined only by incorrect breathing has formed. New and more symptoms add, thanks to hyperventilation and blood saturation with oxygen. A series of reactions is set going and for its recovery the organism needs a lot of time after a panic attack, sometimes long hours. Fear is permanently established in the mind.

As soon as I started feeling the coming panic, I was starting breathing „through the abdomen". It is good to focus even only on how the abdomen moves, how you breathe in and breathe out. This distracting will slightly take you away from the panic situation. While breathing, you can also close your eyes and start repeating to yourself: „I am calm! I am calm!" Be confident in what you pronounce! Breathe, look around – there is nothing threatening your life. Relax and look objectively at the surrounding environment. Towards what is happening at the moment around you. There is nothing frightening.

When you have good understanding in your mind about what happens during attack, anxiety reduces and the fear that strains your mind and body, stops. The natural process of breathing is not disturbed and the panic attack does not unlock and is not fed at body level. The important thing in this case is to be aware what happens, that nothing actually threatens us, and to keep our normal breathing. To keep calm and the panic would pass us by.

With me, the panic attacks started becoming less frequent in the course of time and used to occur only when I travelled by car long way and when I flew by plane. But they were fearful enough, I just freaked out. Even at the thought of an urgent travelling I started getting sick and difficult to breathe. It was somewhat easier in a car because I knew I could get off almost any time, but in a plane... how to say it... panic not just seized me but took hold of the whole world, at least the one that I could see. It was terrifying. I wanted to travel and to overcome my fear. I felt as if in a trap in that small closed space and the lack of way out in case I'd wish for, drove me crazy. I was trembling, crying, I prayed, I cried again during all my trips, and I was dying of fear throughout the whole trip, literally. I didn't dare to take tranquillizing medication, because I was seized by the fear they would cause something irretrievable, I would get asleep and wouldn't be able to wake up anymore, and they have no way to help me at such a place. I didn't dare to drink alcohol because I was afraid I'd choke or would get drunk, or would faint and there would be nobody to help. Crazy, isn't it? The good news is that nobody has ever died of a panic attack, except mentally.

I didn't have any worries of flying by plane before the occurrence of my new psychological torment. I have flown on my own in the skies, without any acquaintances or relatives, to the United States. It is quite a distance, but I didn't bother. It was something normal, even boring.

Control

I have flown once a year by plane at long distances in the last four years. I dare to say, yet last year I overcame my fear completely and my time in that machine passes smoothly. I realized I can't control the situation I am in, but I can control my own thoughts. ***The only control is the one upon our own thoughts*** and the way we perceive what is happening around us. ***And it is our thoughts that create our reality.*** Neither people, nor situations could be put under our control. It is crucial for everybody to realize that and to leave things around him happen the way the Devine has assigned. You are only required to believe. **To believe** that when you expect the best for you, then sooner or later, it will come. Let the Universe take care how it would happen.

The trap we fall in, originates from the inability to control. Not ourselves but the surrounding environment. We don't see way out because we have walled it up with fear. Let your mind at ease,

learn not to worry unduly and if problems come around, you can always solve them with sober mind. Without fear. I know it sounds banal and easy in words but it would happen by continuous practice. **Habits might change in subconsciousness.**

One more interesting detail is that years ago, before these states seized me; I had decided to make a tattoo. It had to be an inscription, saying „Without fear" in English. I was fearless at the time. How ironic! I already pay quite an attention to the signs of fate, or call it whatever you like, but there are definitely no accidental things.

I am completely sure these panic attacks happened to me in order to teach me something. They made me halt and pay attention to myself. I still do it, I try to make my needs and wishes priority. I conform only to my children but it is no good for them to teach them one should put somebody else's needs before his own. Everything and everybody could wait. Even if it is pressing. **Patience is crucial for building a stable mental peace.** We can't get everything we want and when we want it. I try to teach that my children, too.

The ability to postpone the satisfaction of needs is one of the factors for future success. Otherwise we make our children happy only at the very moment and unsatisfied in the long term. Gradually, our children become less prepared to cope with even less stressful situations, which eventually turns into quite an obstacle for their success in life.

We often witness the child's inability to postpone its desires when hearing „No". Because parents have tamed its brain to get right away everything it wants. Today children are obsessed by mobile equipment and games. Each on-line battle, each victory enhances the dopamine level and acts as drug on them. It addicts them. ***Pleasure always addicts.* Dopamine** is substance that is responsible for motivation and concentration. By modern technologies, children do not have motivation any more, they concentrate difficultly and are constantly dull. And how it'd be else as far as you have in your hands a flow of pleasure that acts directly on your nervous system?

Actually, my panic fear was drawn a little bit aside alongside the cares for my children while being babies. I didn't have time for anything and when I did have some free time, I used it to sleep. And mostly, because I lived in the present. My dream had become true and I didn't look at the past. The love for my children changed me, too. ***It is important for your thoughts to be exactly where your body is at the same moment.*** Live consciously at each very moment! ***Be present!***

When one does not live „here and now", he is unconscious person led by stereotyped habits. Have you noticed how children enjoy everything, how they live for the moment? This happens before we load them with our understandings about the world. Their consciousness is present in the surrounding environment. They observe, examine, admire, enjoy. It has always been interesting to me with my children as far as I have direct observations on them, how they give names to the things they do. For example: „I climb up the steps", „I drink water", „I go to the restroom". Perhaps this naming of things we do, keeps us at the present moment.

Another thing that has helped me is the *instantaneous distracting*. When I feel the panic is coming, I find an occupation in order to stay in my previous mental situation. As far as panic used to find me most often in a car, I right away gripped the mobile and started reviewing my messages or looked for somebody to call for a talk. The support of helping distraction acts pretty usefully. If there is nobody to share with or to tell your worries, I am available. I am giving my contact details for connection with me in the end of the book. I will make a closed group in social media in order to be able to connect there. **You can contact me if in need of distracting, sharing, support and understanding.**

Never forget that this state of yours is not deadly. Your heart won't stop and you don't suffer a terminal disease, just adrenaline is little bit more in your body. **Adrenaline is a hormone.** It is also called a hormone of stress because of the fact adrenaline synthesis accelerates significantly in stressful situations such as fear, anger, danger, physical efforts, etc. Adrenaline basic role is to prepare the organism for coping with the arisen situation. It also influences the emotional condition. If it doesn't continue for too long, this flow of energy could be good thing. According to some authors each person has his own norm of emotions, the so called emotional peak, which reaching the person needs from time to time. The inability for such an act may lead to development of depression. The hormone of stress should not unlock for a longer time in our body. When the cause of stress does not go away, you may experience chronic anxiety and pressure similar to an engine that is constantly put on high speeds. That's why the ability to cope with stress is important for your physical as well as mental health.

The Reactions to Stress

Hans Selye describes the reactions to stress in the 40s of the last century. According to him, organism's reaction to stress is the same despite of the type of stressor (positive or negative). The initial phase is **alarm**. It progresses within 6-48 hours after the stressing event and engages the nervous system. The heartbeat and the blood pressure increase. The next phase is **resistance**, where still more adrenaline releases and the production of other hormones (e.g. the hormone of growth) reduces. If the stressor is not big, the body returns to its normal functioning. The third phase is **exhaustion**, where in case of continuous stress the body loses its power to resist. Here affections manifest as result of the experienced stress.

Stress reduces the immune system's ability to fight bacteria and viruses that occupy our body. The immune system fights diseases by producing **lymphocytes**.

__________________To start believing...

These cells bind with bacteria and viruses and destroy them. At stress, the lymphocytes production reduces and the body finds it more difficult to cope with the disease. The lack of lymphocytes makes people pliable to diseases, they are already liable to, e.g. asthma and eczema. The following immune system diseases are considered due to or intensified by stress: allergies, arthritis, multiple sclerosis, rheumatoid arthritis, veal-skin, etc.

Chronic stress leads also to increased blood coagulability. Beside the direct consequences for the cardiovascular system, which lead in the long run to diseases like high blood pressure, heart coronary disease, heart attacks and strokes, there are also indirect ones. They are connected with using non-adaptive mechanisms for coping with stress such as smoking and alcohol abuse, which themselves are a risk factor for the occurrence of cardiovascular diseases. Some of the cardiovascular system diseases, which are flatly connected to stress, are: arteriosclerosis, essential hypertension, Buerger's disease, Raynaud's disease, tachycardia, etc.

Each listing of diseases like that does not act positively on the mind, but my goal is to make you re-think what you cause to

your body by the constant stress we make it subject to. Yes, no one dies of panic attacks, be sure of that, because there is not such registered case yet. You could be the first... don't be afraid, this was joke. Panic crises do not cause death, but if they start occurring way often, they start damaging organism's cells.

Stress on its own is not obligatory damaging. The American Psychological Association notes: „Stress reminds of stretching a violin's string: if it's not well stretched, the sound would be hollow and scraping, and if it's way too stretched, the sound would be sharp or the string would tear. Stress could be deadly or could make our life exciting. The point is how to master it."

In order to fight the constant stress some people resort to alcohol, drugs or cigarettes. Others start eating unbalanced or remain long at the TV or computer.

Stress is responsible for 90 % of the diseases in the organism. Chronic fear causes anomalies in the body. Change your way of thinking and you'd change the chemical reactions.

Life is not given us by inheritance, we ourselves create it. The key that controls our biology is called perception. It sounds unbelievable to you? If diseases occur by inheritance, then why don't they manifest at certain interval and don't progress the same way?

———————————————To start believing...

Because the surrounding environment, the feelings, the reactions, our perception varies.

The new biology science is the „**epigenetics**". *The fate of cells in the organism does not depend on the genes but on the way we perceive what happens around us.* How, otherwise, would you explain the fact that identical twins are born with almost the same genes but their lives flow and finish in different ways? The answer is hidden in the environment we are subject to and the brain's reaction to it. Perception is something we believe in. Genes and behaviour are defined by our beliefs. *People are born with certain genes but they can change the way these genes are being read.* Only a small part of the genes in the DNA cannot be modified, and the rest are subject to change. About 1 % – 2 % of diseases are due to bad genes, and the rest are caused by our thoughts, actions, emotions, choices, etc.

Perhaps, all of you have heard of, and why not experienced, the „placebo effect ". The placebo (comfort) effect is a phenomenon, where a patient's symptoms may improve at the presence of unsuccessful or false treatment only because the patient believes he'd recover or that the treatment helps him, despite the medicinal point of view. From a scientific point of view, homeopathy is example of a placebo effect.

Perception controls the genes and this is Faith.

A person may live in a peaceful environment but even though to perceive it as hostile. Our cells do not react to the environment but to our interpretation of it.

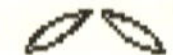

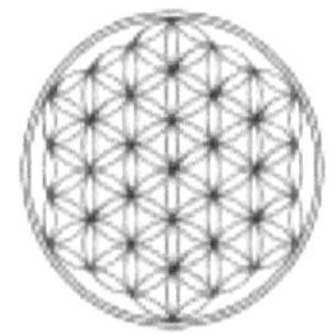

Consciousness and Unconsciousness

We can reset our genes through our consciousness and faith.
Buddha has said: „We turn in what we think".

Perception is defined by our mind. It is entity of
Consciousness and **Unconsciousness.** Conscious mind
reflects our wishes and strivings. It is our source of identity.
Unconsciousness is mechanism for recording and recalling,
which consists of habits and programmes that are acquired
from the family and environment. Up to 70 % of these
programmes are destructive. When you are ready and you
wish for standing against your weaknesses, to change the
negative programming inside you and to transfer it to positive
according your views, then you will start uncovering the
abundance of life.

Many people cannot be helped because you can't help
somebody, who doesn't want the change himself. *Each person
should set the mechanisms in his body going himself in order
to change his life.* One should realize the connection between

thought and conditions. One provokes all that happens to him himself. Both, good as well as evil. We can't blame anyone else for our own fate, nor pretend we are victims.

According to some scientific researches in the field of neurobiology, we spent 95 % of the day in thinking, while our behaviour is preconditioned by our unconsciousness at the time. The unconsciousness is comprised of programmed behaviour. Magnetoencephalography studies show that the brain vibrates at certain frequency and what we radiate, this is what comes back to us. This is the way we create our own reality.

This means that if we've grown up in a poor family, perhaps we'd be poor in the future as well. It is the same if we have grown in a family, where quarrels happen often, then, perhaps, we'd attract similar events in our life. This is due to the programmes in the unconsciousness, formed in the period from 0 to 7 years of age. It is in this period that the brain records everything it observes in the environment. This is of quite a significance in educational aspect. *The accumulated life experience is stored in the unconsciousness in the form of a programme/habit.* Automatic reactions are action of the unconsciousness, while consciousness analyzes the surrounding environment it sees. Children's brain in the first seven years functions at low frequencies, characteristic of deep hypnosis.

_______________To start believing...

Walking, breathing, writing, reading, driving a car – these all are habits we have built in the unconsciousness and we do them automatically. The built habits form our character.

Don't be in a hurry to reproach yourself. What we missed to do in the first seven years or we have perceived wrongly, we can change at each stage of our development. We can do the transition to consciousness through the power of our knowledge and faith. „Until we don't turn the unconscious conscious, it would rule our life and we'd continue calling it fate", remember well these words of C. G. Jung.

The programming of unconsciousness is building of new habits or changing old ones. It consumes time and efforts on your behalf. It is similar to learning new matter. It has to be read many times in order to realize it, to learn it and then to start practicing it. It took me about two-three years but the first two I was looking primarily for information and the next year I was applying the learned on myself.

No one of us feels complete safety. As the Bible says: „time and unprecedented come to all of us ". How then to overcome the feeling of insecurity? Try the following suggestions:

• Share your feelings with relative or friend worthy trust. Researches point that close ones'

support ensures constant protection from diseases due to stress. Yes, "the true friend loves all the time and is brother, born for the times of trouble".

• Do not constantly expect the worst. It would only exhaust you emotionally. What you are afraid of could never happen! It is with a reason that the Bible says: „Don't you ever worry about tomorrow because tomorrow would bring its own worry".

(Proverbs 17:17, Bible BG)

• Try to preserve your composure when somebody makes you angry. Don't add fuel to the flames.

„Soft answer subdues fury, and the offensive word provokes anger".

(Proverbs 15:1, Bible BG)

• Try to smooth over the differences with the other one in private and with respect. Try to forgive. To forgive is not only beautiful but also useful for the health. According to a study held in 2001, when a person does not forgive, it leads to significant increase of blood pressure and heartbeat, while forgiveness reduces stress.

Have faith. In everything and mainly in yourself. ***The key to peaceful living is inside you.*** Unlock the door, don't lock it up. Surround yourself with people, whose energy does not burden you but makes you feel nicely and safely. Avoid acquaintances and relatives, who strain your

mind. Don't think about them and their actions. ***Be egoists in order to preserve yourselves.***

I mentioned earlier that people, who get panic attacks, are at quite an intellectual level. Mentally limited person does not think, he acts after else's commands.

Excessive considering worsens the things with psychic states inside the organism. I don't intend to defend a doctor's degree or to make medicinally competent statement. My observations and conclusions are from talks and studies with people, who have experienced panic and this, not just once, but multiple times.

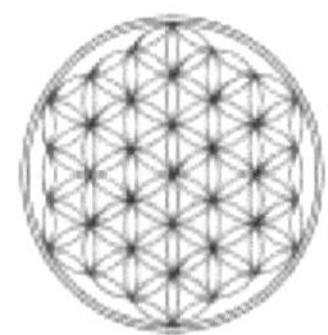

Emotional Intelligence

Now I want to draw your attention to and to acquaint you with the emotional intelligence because it is important to strive doing good. Kindness would bring you humbleness and humbleness would unlock harmony and balance in life.

What is understood under **emotional intelligence** is the ability or the skill to perceive, evaluate and manage own emotions, to differentiate various emotions and to name and define them correctly as well as to use emotional information in order to manage thinking and behaviour through it. This is comparatively new field of psychological study.

The idea of emotional intelligence appears for the first time yet in the early works of Charles Darwin in regard to emotions expression's significance for surviving and adaptation. In the first decade of the 20th century, although traditional intelligence definitions attribute particular meaning to cognitive aspects as memory and problems solving, some influential researchers in the field of intelligence start

recognizing the significance of the non-cognitive aspect.

According to positive psychology, emotional intelligence is one of the 6 known virtues and 24 powers for happiness. It is connected with the human ability to maintain relations of respect and love with people, who surround him and with whom he communicates.

Their description below follows the structure of a piece from the book „Positive Psychology" by Dr. Roselyn Bloom:

6 virtues

Virtues are fascinating characteristics that ensure moral perfection. The present six virtues could be found in most cultures around the world.

- Wisdom and Knowledge
- Courage
- Humanity
- Justice
- Moderation
- Transcendence

According to positive psychology, if a person develops these six virtues and their relevant powers in him, he would increase happiness and meaning of his life.

24 powers

There are various ways towards acquiring each of the six virtues. In positive psychology, these ways are called „powers". Practically, the powers are skills and everybody could acquire one or another power.

1. *Wisdom and Knowledge*

- Creativity – to invent new ways of action;
- Curiosity – to uncover world;
- Breadth of mind, critical thought and self-establishing – to observe people and phenomena from all aspects;
- Satisfaction from studying – to master new knowledge;
- Sense of perspective and prudence – to analyze the situation sidelong.

1. *Courage*

- Sincerity and honesty – to be ourselves and to dare saying what we think;
- Determination – to take the challenges and to stand against difficulties;
- Constancy – to complete what's begun;
- Enthusiasm and optimism – to dive into life and to cheerfully watch reality.

1. Humanity

- Kindness and generosity – to do good around us;
- Love – to attribute significance to intimate and private relations;
- Emotional intelligence – to become aware of emotions.

1. Justice

- Detachment – to have the same attitude towards everybody;
- Team spirit and loyalty – to cooperate with the others and to work in a team;
- Leadership – to organize group activities.

1. Moderation

- Sympathy and forgiveness – to truly hear the others;
- Modesty and humbleness – to not strive to make brilliant display by all means;
- Patience, cautiousness and steadiness – to think before acting;
- Self-control – to be masters of ourselves.

6. Transcendence

- Evaluation of beauty and perfection – to see and to appreciate;
- Gratitude and appreciation – to be aware of good that happens to us;
- Hope – to observe the future with faith;
- Laugh and smile – to have fun and to focus on humour;
- Faith and spirituality – to live with the feeling life does make sense.

Positive psychology directs to the idea that if we systematically strive for the better and we daily cover certain part of the road to improvement, in the long run, we'd get closer to the state, where we'd be more complete and hence happier personalities.

The emotionally intelligent person distinguishes his emotions and uses them to direct his consciousness and actions. Everybody is able to improve his emotional intelligence. For that purpose, we need to work for the development of **five skills**:

- Self-awareness – clearness about our feelings and opinions; ability to use our instinct and intuition in order to guide our solutions; skill to judge ourselves justly and to believe ourselves.

_______________To start believing...

- Self-regulation – talent to control our emotions; patience and not expecting immediate reward for our efforts; ability to quickly recover after emotional confusion.
- Motivation – to do what we love; to let the strivings of ours lead us; to persevere despite the difficulties.
- Empathy – ability to change our opinion; the ability to set ourselves at the place of the other party and to understand his/her thoughts, feelings, moods and behaviour; to maintain calm and stimulating relations with various people.
- Social skills – ability to master our own emotions in the relations with others; the ability to comprehend what happens around us regarding human relations; ability to smooth differences, to negotiate, to cooperate in a team.

Practical Steps

Learn how to master your emotions. Fear is emotion, happiness is one, too. Let us try to exchange the negative emotion for a positive one. That elevated feeling of happiness everybody looks for. It is inside us. Nobody and nothing material could make you happy before uncovering that ***happiness is inside you***. Once you find it, you will start radiating it. You would not be vulnerable for external aggressors and negative energies that strange people would transfer to you.

I was about 30 years old, when I met death. I couldn't see it but I felt it. There were problems with giving birth to my children and something happened in my organism. The doctors said it was pneumonia but were not firm. Whatever the illness was I only knew I couldn't breathe, I was stopping breathing and was losing consciousness. I was put on artificial aspiration for two-three days. I could hardly inhale, I couldn't move, didn't hear, didn't see. Nothing mattered. I didn't feel any fear. It was so serene...

________________________To start believing...

People, it was serene... the feeling was of a great serenity. While lying in that condition, I felt someone started shaking me a way strongly. I opened my eyes and saw a nurse, who was saying something to me. I only heard her telling me the following: „If you don't try to get up, you would never ever see your children!" These words got me back to reality, I knew I shouldn't surrender, the time to leave hadn't come. I started feeling the pain, too – physical and mental. I was alive!

Motivation is necessary, strong desire for life and evaluation of your actions in order to help yourself starting getting over the panic attacks. Death is not frightening, the frightening is to die every day and not to appreciate the life you have been given. This is the biggest wealth. My favourite part of the day is the morning, when everything starts again and you are given a priceless gift – the opportunity to enjoy small things, to take care of beloved people, to improve yourself, to get to know yourself... to get to know the people around you, to progress, to help and to be useful.

And coffee, of course. In the morning – coffee with milk, if possible, cappuccino. Small but great pleasures. I wake up early in the morning in order to make coffee. I read things I am interested in and make plan for the day.

What a percentage of you start your day with analyzing problems, review of past events that have hurt us and with experiencing again the same emotions? Let me guess? Great percentage of you! And this is quite a mistake. Past emotions you've come across transform in future experiences. Thus your day would proceed the same way, you would do the same things and would feel miserable.

***Love yourself and show it to yourself.* Respect yourself.** Do not undertake actions that don't correspond with your inner convictions. It would stress you. And our goal is to reduce stress, the factors that provoke it, and anxiety. Each problem would solve with or without your involvement. Do not do everything at any cost. Appreciate your time and use it reasonably. Do not waste it in self-accusations and picturing scenarios what could happen. If you have made your efforts to master a crisis situation and there was no effect, don't get angry, don't accuse yourself. Don't bother but proceed ahead. You did what depended on you.

The desire to collect my knowledge and experience in a book occurred after my views for the world changed. Yes, after the panic disorder occurrence and my desire to be a better person. I want to share my experience and to be useful for other people. I'd be happy if I help at least one of you. I'd be satisfied if something out of what is described here, makes you re-think things or gives you direction how to overtake stress and, why not, to find the way of healing.

I won't lie, I still learn, but I am already happy. ***Dream!*** Outline dreams for yourself. Something you have always wanted or have postponed. And start working on your goals. Every day. With constancy, will, patience and respect.

Until your thought doesn't bond with ***a goal***, you cannot take advantage of spiritual healing. You need a goal to be in the centre of your thought every day. The goals define the way of thinking, and the way of thinking changes the conditions success depends on.

I acquired new perspective to the surrounding environment as well as the ability to peer at the signs I am given.

I am to describe few ***preventive measures*** through which you to start reducing your panic seizures. You have to reduce them to such a level for them to start happening very rarely and for short. I hope all of you already know that you won't die during a panic attack. Seen from another point of view, death is not frightening. Sooner or later it comes for everybody but do your best to live your life calmly and to take advantage of everything Universe can offer you. It is meant for you and is awaiting you somewhere. Only ask for it! Be brave! Live! Everybody deserves only the best and everybody is responsible for it, to work on the way he wants to live. Now someone would tell me: super, it is easy to say it.

I know it is easy to say it, but I also know what hard work it requires to do it. I don't want to live an easy way, without goals, without development, without strivings. It is also very easy to constantly complain, to blame somebody else or to excuse ourselves. What is easy, does not lead to progress. **You should make your best in order to be the person you'd like to be.** Don't you try to be what someone else or the society expects you to be. ***Be yourself!*** The biggest excuse is that no time is the right one for change. We constantly wait something to pass, something to happen, somebody to come. There is nothing like that. Either, there isn't such time. **The moment is here and now.** Exactly that short moment, while you are reading the present. Start the change with yourself. Write on a sheet of paper what you want to do, what you want to achieve from now on. After deciding to write your wishes on a sheet of paper, did it turn a hard task to formulate them precisely? Hard because we don't actually know what we want, that's why we don't get it. We are in constant denial with ourselves and often use phrases starting with „No": I don't want, I can't, the time is not now, I don't deserve. Stop putting own limitations. Unfold that potential.

I am sure everybody wants to live better. Start living better. Change the job you don't like. Change the place of living, the people around you. Change everything you dislike. What are you saying? You have no opportunity? You have no job? There is job. Do you have qualification for better job? No. Study then, educate yourself some more. Educate yourself continuously. **Knowledge and information are the most precious resource for progress.** Find the thing you are the best in, your talent, and work. Perhaps the money you'd earn wouldn't be cosmic sum but the satisfaction of the completed work is well worth. The calmness it brings. The big wealth is not a ticket for the rocket of success. It won't fire you to heaven. Let's forget greed. But don't underestimate yourself. What you give as labour and efforts should be reciprocal to what you are paid. The more efforts you made, the bigger income you'd have.

If you still have no goals, then write on a sheet of paper all thoughts and feelings that come to your mind at the moment. Without reproaching yourself for neither of them. Accept them with love and start slowly transforming them into positive ones. Patience is necessary. Each change starts with understanding,

acceptance of the old and readiness for new one. You cannot start something new if you haven't *accepted and forgiven* the old experiences. Do not give up! Your efforts would be rewarded! Be sure in achieving your goal! Feel the change, the relief, as if they are already true, and start believing in that.

Be patient, repeat yourself what you want and visualize the picture in your mind. Whatever picture for yourself and for the world you have in your mind, the brain reads it and reproduces it as interior biochemistry it saturates the body with in order to be able to reproduce the picture. Our genetics is controlled similar way.

Also change is necessary in the following vital daily things:

✓ Full-fledged sleep.

✓ Walking in fresh air.

✓ Regular but not excessive and burdening exercising.

✓ Denial of or reduced intake of energy drinks, smoking and alcohol.

✓ Proper nutrition and consumption of more vitamins.

✓ Less time on internet, TV, in order to exclude negative emotions.

✓ Avoid and do not participate in arguments, stressful situations.

✓ Walks in the nature or in the open.

✓ Working day's reasonable distribution.

✓ Rest.

✓ Meditation, yoga.

I am trying a type of meditation techniques upon myself for few days already. It acts very well on me and relaxes me. I'll share in order you to try. I am an absolute laic in meditation and I am just to dive into its matter.

Before starting the meditation, you need to save some 30 minutes, during which nobody would disturb and engage you. The best time is in the morning, a little after waking up, or in the evening before falling asleep. It is good for the room to be dimmed out at the no presence of side noises. With me it happens best in the evening. Choose a calming melody from internet, set it for 30–40 minutes in order not to consider how much time's passed. Once the melody finishes, it's time to open eyes with ease.

You should experience no hunger, thirst, not to be cold – generally, to be in physical comfort. Ensconce yourself comfortably. You might be lying or sitting but with stretched back in order to avoid falling asleep if you are too relaxed. Let your palms be directed upwards.

Play the melody, close your eyes, take a deep breath „through the stomach", hold it and breathe out smoothly. Count your breathings in after which concentrate totally on breathing. Feel the air getting in and out through your body, fill it up with love. From time to time a single thought would sneak in your mind.

Don't let this disturb you, register it and let it go without analyzing it. Don't think about it and don't you think that you shouldn't think. Relax. With your eyes closed, imagine the darkness you see. Peer into it and see how it becomes darker and wider. You could imagine the Cosmos or the endless Universe and how you dip into it. The goal is to come to meditative repose and to detach from your thoughts. Focus on darkness and your head. Feel them. Your task is only to observe, without reproaching or judging some events that might arise during the meditation. They are past – accept them with love. Change the negative feelings with calmness and acceptance. Release yourself from the past feelings.

There is probability to remember events connected with aggression, insult, pain and misadventure. Something that has traumatized you psychically. Do not avoid these memories but try to accept them and to „cure" from them. Accept them with understanding and love. ***Show yourself you love yourself and that there is no way for something past to harm you.*** This would bring you great relief. You'd need, of course, patience.

When I learned a little bit of casting aside my thoughts during that meditation, I started sensing kind of serene feeling, while my consciousness was roaming without direction and goal.

The other thing I like is that I start experiencing kind of tingling on my palms. It is perhaps energy that could be sensed.

When the melody finishes, open slowly your eyes. I hope you'd feel satisfaction. Practice this type of meditation often. Not as an obligation but as an experience towards your essence.

I started doing physical exercises at home few years ago. Light ones, not burdening. It turned out to be much boring and I didn't have motivation to go on. I had gained considerable weight after giving birth to my children but I didn't pay attention to that. I have twins, a boy and a girl. The most wonderful children that I had wished for and they came true. Along the care for them, while they were babies, I didn't have time at all; neither had I had the desire to deal much with my appearance. Children grew up, I started going out, I kind of renewed a little bit my social life. I had had dinner on a venue and an acquaintance of mine sent me a picture from that evening. Hardly then I realized how I look like and that I don't want to look like this. Until that very moment, I staffed myself with literally any garbage, at any time of day and night. Cakes, croissants, chocolate, éclairs and much other useless food. I stopped consuming sweet at once. Decided today and started the next day. I didn't taste sweet things for six months.

I went in for fitness. I practiced with the help of an instructor for about a month in order to direct me to the correct performance of basic exercises. After that, I continued on my own. I found how well these trainings act on me. Even if I went to the fitness unwilling sometimes, because of the early hour, after the training I felt charged with power. This is the feeling short physical exercising brings. Not aiming to build up muscles but to maintain the circulation of blood within the norm. Obligatory start training something, whatever it is. ***Take care of your body with love and gratitude.*** There are a lot of group sports today, if you are not fan of individual trainings in the fitness. I personally like most the trainings with apparatuses in the fitness. I even like them so much that I have set as a goal to open my own fitness club one day. Private club, where all of you would be invited to charge your body with hormones of happiness. In the course of time, I decided I don't want to be only a fitness club but a small health centre. A place, where people feeling in a dead-lock and having to make change but needing support and direction would come. I will do it one day, when I have the necessary financial resource.

Physical exercises bring me joy, make me relaxed and relieved. Alongside with fitness, I go

to the park. Biking, running... choose something but obligatory train. I promise that beside benefits for your appearance, training would charge you with spiritual energy also.

Full-fledged sleep is very significant for your body. Under the generalized term of „body" I mean unity of physical body, organs, brain activity and all the rest we are built of. You need at least seven hours of sleep, no matter what time you go to bed. The important is your organism to be able to have rest and recharge.

Try to go to bed at the same time. The body will get used to the routine and you'll start feeling sleepy automatically. You need to set your inner clock.

Many years ago, I worked at the reception of a hotel. My work was on shifts, day and night ones. In the course of the four years I worked this way, my biological clock had disarranged. I started having problems with memory and concentration. I still have memory problems today. I have perhaps destroyed an important part of my brain activity.

The most important part of your life change is connected namely with the sleep. Or more precisely, with that short period of time just before the moment of falling asleep. At this very moment, you have the power to redirect your unconsciousness and to start changing your life. Habits are built in the unconsciousness and they manage the things unconsciously happening around and with you. I want here you to already start reading very carefully. Re-read even. Try to perform it for at least two months.

Daily. You will start feeling difference in your perceptions and will start finding the light to lead you along the way. You will find stimulus to wake up in the morning and to start your creative processes. You will charge with new energy that will give you strengths to think, to undertake risks, to fight for, to work, to put all your energy and soul in what you aim. And what do you aim? You have to set a goal. **It is time for you to get out of the notorious comfort zone, to stop sailing along the stream and to start progressing.** You have to be the best version of yours. The one you will build in your mind yourself. What a person would you like to be? Every evening before falling asleep, imagine the way you'd like to look, what you'd like to work, the love, if you miss it (how the dreamed partner looks like), where you'd like to live and generally, all that makes you happy. Thus, you will state your wishes before you inner Self and will programme them in your unconsciousness. Once the habit is set in your unconsciousness, the consciousness will start striving towards fulfilling the goals. The goals, of course, should be precise. You need to excellently know what and how you want it in order not to get something different. And not only that. You have to put the right emotion, when visualizing your goals. If you'd like to be in love, then imagine the emotion this

feeling would bring. Imagine the happiness, the gratitude, the butterflies in the stomach, the delight. Once you feel the emotion in your mind, then tell yourself even aloud: „I am in love!" You have to show your body what to look for, what vibration to send to the Universe. You cannot wish for love, while your unconsciousness remembers the bad memory from your last love affair. You will get the same because this is the emotion your consciousness looks for. This is the reason for many dreams to fail or we believe we had wished for something and it came true but not the right way.

Strange or not, but this is the way I made my dream to have twins – a boy and a girl – come true. I already shared I had problem with getting pregnant. The happy news wasn't coming for several months in a row. Despite the hard moments, filled with discourage and tears, I didn't stop believing in the miracle. **Faith is what gives us strength to go on, when things seem hopeless.** I kept being sure each next month is my month. About a year passed within that expectation. Somewhere there my panic attacks disappeared, too. I was falling asleep in the evening with the thought that I would have children soon. I wanted twins, a boy and a girl. The girl to have her father's eyes, and the boy to be alike me.

I started making any possible tests, which took weeks. I was taking numerous pills, I was injected various things, I was even transfused a serum. I was thrilled expecting the happy news each month, and when I was seeing the negative pregnancy test, I burst in tears. But my faith didn't leave me, for the test would be positive. The month before knowing that I am finally pregnant, I was on my regular examination at the gynecologist's. Getting out of his room, I stated: „Doc, I am getting pregnant this month! With twins!" He smiled and said: „I wish for succeeding getting you pregnant with just one, you dream of two..."

I had an icon of Saint Virgin Mary hanging on the wall at home; I had got it as a gift. Sometimes, before falling asleep, I was saying a prayer of gratitude along with my desire to get a boy and a girl. March was coming. The year 2012. On March, 25th I heard I am pregnant. The Annunciation. I rushed with the test because I was impatient, and I saw a vague dash that was only hinting for pregnancy. I would even say, I used my imagination to see it, but it was there. I went for a blood test in few days because I wanted to be flatly sure the test was correct.

So, it could seem to you strange, funny, even accidental coincidence. But the facts are

facts. Now I have the most gorgeous children, despite the misadventures I experienced. Just what I wished them to be. This is how my dearest wish came true. Each woman, who wishes for a child but has difficulties to get pregnant, would understand me. The faith helped me to go on and to realize my dream. It took me time but I didn't give up, because I believed and I knew it is matter of time the things to happen. I knew exactly what I want and I was ready to do anything necessary in order that fantasy to turn into reality. I was not waiting but acting!

I again have a goal and a plan now I am working on. I act the same way and I hope to share with you in a while whether I have succeeded. I believe in myself! You, too, start believing in your own abilities!

Let me tell you about unconsciousness and its role for the change of way of life.

Unconsciousness is like a recording device. It stores programmes you've been born with – controlling breathing, the heartbeat and all other functions you have established yourself – such as the way you walk, talk, write, dance, drive, etc.

New programmes are established easiest before children round seven years. That's why the expression "the first seven years are most important" is so popular. In the course of these years the programmes in the unconsciousness are formed, the person's habits. Till the age of seven

children are like an opened book and absorb new information with ease. Brain waves of children are different: they are slower and this is why children live at the present moment. They use their imagination. They dream. Children do not have filters. This explains why you can irreversibly slow down a child's progress by telling it it's stupid. Whatever you tell a three-year old child – „You are wonderful", „You are special", „Nothing will come out of you", „You make mom unhappy" – everything turns into a rule for it. The continuous repeating of these definitions get into the child's unconsciousness and they turn into truth.

There are 5 major frequencies of brain waves – Beta, Alpha, Gamma, Theta and Delta. Everything we say and think regulates the brain waves' frequencies.

Beta – 12 to 30 Hz

The brain waves in the *Beta frequency bandwidth* belong to our normal awake consciousness. This is connected watchfulness, logical thinking, problems solving, concentration and other active brain activities. You are in this very state of consciousness also while practicing a sport and talking with other people.

The higher levels of Beta could be result of stress, excitement or restlessness. Although you should be in Beta consciousness in order to perform your usual daily activities, many people are at the higher frequencies connected to stress.

Alpha – 7 to 12 Hz

The Alpha brain waves are slower in frequency compared to Beta and that's why they naturally provide calmer consciousness. The state of consciousness is often observed with people, who are naturally calm. As if you'd like to dream or when you close your eyes in order to meditate. This frequency encourages imagination, memory, concentration, creativity, and reduces stress, which is beneficial to studying.

Meditation supports raising the Alpha frequencies in the brain and the ability to maintain that in the daily activities. With the children there are usually more Alpha waves observed compared to the adults.

Theta – 4 to 7 Hz

The Theta brain waves are observed in deep relaxation and meditation, light sleep. This is also the place, where unconscious mind is active and you are in a state to reach deep insights and intuition. This is the consciousness, where we reach higher universal insights that might change our life.

It sounds controversial but the lower the brain waves are, the easier studying is. Theta is the consciousness, where visualizations, inspiration and creativity are powerful. Meditation and yoga are often praised as useful, because they generate these theta frequencies in the brain. Many people have also paranormal experiences, because of the higher sensibility during theta.

To overcome the destroying effect of thought, you need to find positives even in the most hopeless situations in order not to send negative energy streams. After you have accepted the situation you have popped into, you are to understand it and accept it. I hope I succeeded in explaining summarized enough what the panic attacks are, what the symptoms are and what damages they do on the cells in our body.

Fear and stress could be exchanged with love and calmness. They all are emotions you need to teach your mind to. You have allowed fear to settle in your mind voluntarily or involuntarily and to start thinking you are in a dead end. *There is way out and the choice is inside you. Choose to take responsibility for your own existence and to save yourself from the chains of these negative emotions.* And be patient and assiduous because it will take time. Accept what happened to you with gratitude and

prepare to outline your new life. Choose what you want to be, what you want to happen to you, how you'd like to progress professionally and everything you dream of. Set yourself particular and real goals. Goals should not be far unreal for you, because there would not be a way to believe in them. It is good to have one major goal and several small ones, which to be steps toward the big one. Thus, achieving each small goal will give you confidence on the road to the final result.

Imagine and feel how successful and satisfied you'd like to be in life. Visualize your idea and the feeling that accompanies it. Think of the idea every single evening just before falling asleep and every single morning just when waking up. Before going to sleep, pronounce loudly several encouraging words for the coming new day. For example, how much you love yourself, how grateful you are and how fear does not exist in you. Imagine that beautiful feeling, when somebody gives you a present. This is gratitude. Fill up your mind with it, when sending your wishes to the Universe.

Brain acts at low frequencies during these short moments just before your body sinks into sleep and it is the ideal moment to set new habits in your unconsciousness. And then leave

the Universe to take care of them becoming true.

You want to be happy? Great! What makes you happy? Gratitude, calmness, aspirations. You are happy, when you live for the moment. Concentrate on the activity you are performing at the moment. Look around. Happiness is the focus on the present situation. Each moment that has already passed, doesn't matter, and thinking about it, you distract from your particular goal. There is nothing to be afraid of. Least of death. It seems frightening because it is unknown. The fear from death stops our desire for life. And the latter is so beautiful, mysterious, unexpected, and full of turns and happy moments. Allow yourself to experience them. Relax, you won't die! Don't burden your body and don't waste time, during which you could live fully and make your dreams come true. ***Believe! Start believing yourself! You are able to manage with everything!***

And what so much are you afraid of death? Don't you feel uncomfortable that giving in to fear, you damage every cell of your body? ***Think about yourself. There is nobody more important than you.*** Take care of the coziness in your mind by establishing spiritual comfort through positive and confident thoughts. Instead trembling of fear, tremble with joy. Fill that heart with love and see how it would act

back. Trying to run away from fear, we start directly towards it. We become obsessed and our whole life is controlled by fear. We lose control over our thoughts, actions, emotions. We are subordinate only to fear. We run, hide, isolate ourselves with the only hope not to stand up against it. And in the long run, we run into fear, because it has turned into our leading goal. And not only goal. We are fear, our essence associates with fear and vibrates it out. Because fear is outside us, it cannot exist independently in space. We create it and we are responsible for it. We hide and run from ourselves, we are afraid of ourselves. The way you have allowed it to take possession of you, the same way we should eliminate it. Only if we wish, of course. Without our permission freedom cannot be achieved. Who wants to be free?

> Go somewhere in the nature, sit for a while and think over what you'd like to happen to you. Close your eyes and let the puff of wind, the trees and birds saturate your lungs with life and aspiration.

> In the evening, when you go to bed, start imagining how you look like in your best version. Feel the delight of that. Let yourself fall asleep with that blissful feeling. In the morning, when you wake up, write down your goal on a sheet of paper. For example: *I choose happiness! I am incredible! I am resolved to throw off fear!*, as well as any other thing you wish for: new job, new love,

new friend, new journey, new home, child...

If you'd like to throw off fear, you should be profoundly convicted you want it. Your attitude should not contradict your life situation. Your body is already addicted to it and will try to sabotage your mind in any way in order you to go back to the bad happenings. Be patient and set new habits in your mind. **Do not give up!** Fear and stress are pernicious for your body in the long term. Think about yourself and choose change, even if it looks difficult for you, you will make it! If thoughts can make you ill, the same way they can heal. I managed to free from fear. It took time. It happened slowly not because I didn't have the will and faith but because I didn't know many things. I had just started educating myself how and what causes fear, after which I got interested how consciousness works. I got through this situation completely on my own, without any support. I needed some but the surroundings accepted what was happening with the panic attacks rather jokingly. That's why now I would be very glad if I can help other people. You can always contact me if you need. I know how important it is not to feel casted out and helpless. *Believe in yourself!* You choose the way you want your life to pass. You choose what person you to be. Be grateful, good and humble in order to live in harmony and to follow your way determined!

We can't change our lives without changing ourselves first. Wish for the change and start it! Fear is instinct for survival, when facing real threat or enemy. When the enemy is in your head, who are you afraid of? Don't run from him but fight! The fight is against you, which is a big contradiction. ***You decide whether to win or lose!***